Thank you Cyndee for putti been feeling for some time ... the need for more intentional pouring of our faith into the lives of women in our church family and community. *Rethinking Fellowship* brings that breath of fresh air that will provide a strategic means to help ministry teams go deeper with others. So many pages filled with so many ideas. I can't wait to share and pray about implementing them with our team!

—Linda Totman, Women's Ministry Coordinator,
Countryside Covenant Church

I really appreciate the "gentle nudge" to continue to "serve (our) women well while pointing them to Christ" and a closer look at developing those holy habits. The whole book is an easy read full of great information that is sure to have you pulling out your calendar!

—Kristi Bomar, Women's Ministry Co-Leader,
Faith Outreach Christian Center

This is a great resource for those who are seeking to shake things up in their women's church group. It is Biblically sound and provides a wealth of information in an easy-to-understand format to transform your group into a thriving and purposeful arm in your church.

—Cheryl Poulin, Women's Ministry Director,
Christian Life Center, Kent, Ohio

Cyndee's book caused me to pause and think about every women's event our church hosts. Are we remembering to make sure we know our why before we decide on when and how? This book is full of practical tips and ideas which will help me and many others serving in women's ministry.

—Heather Herget, Women's Ministry
Coordinator, FBC Desoto

Cyndee lays out how the planning process should take place—establish your desired outcome first. The goal of the event should be grounded in Scripture and Cyndee provides clear direction for how to establish that foundation. All the examples of events and meeting ideas are the frosting on the cake!

—Barbara Bodley, Women's Ministry Team
Member, Christ's Church at Mason

I have been involved in church work my whole life... The book gave me different perspectives and reinforced my thoughts that our meetings don't need to be fun and games but we need to dig into God's Word... Great book and a great resource for ladies ministry groups that are starting or stale.

—Pharis Copeland, President, Ladies Ministry at
Anchor of Hope Worship Center in Soperton, Georgia

RETHINKING FELLOWSHIP

A HANDBOOK FOR HOSTING MEANINGFUL WOMEN'S MINISTRY EVENTS

CYNDEE OWNBEY

Rethinking Fellowship

ONB Press, Charlotte, NC
Copyright 2023 by Cyndee Ownbey

Cover & interior design by Typewriter Creative Co.
Edited by Thelma Nienhuis

ISBN 978-1-7334710-4-6 (paperback)
ISBN 978-1-7334710-5-3 (ebook)

TABLE OF CONTENTS

INTRODUCTION

THEY SAY A WOMAN CAN NEVER HAVE TOO MANY PURSES OR pairs of shoes. As women's ministry leaders, we know one can never have too many event ideas!

Blank ministry calendars are often the source of anxiety or excitement. The optimist sees each square as an opportunity to do something new and fun for the women in their church. The pessimist dreads the decision-making process.

A recent Google search for "women's ministry event ideas" yielded 3 million results. "Women's fellowship ideas" a whopping 20 million results. Despite the abundance of event and fellowship ideas on the internet and Pinterest, leaders are constantly on the lookout for something new and fresh, something their women will find appealing enough to set aside other obligations and responsibilities to come out for a women's ministry event.

What began as a simple desire to gather a list of women's ministry events and fellowship ideas quickly morphed into a deep dive into fellowship. I found myself wondering: what is fellowship? What's the difference between a gathering in my neighborhood and a women's ministry fellowship activity? Do they look different? Should they look different? How can we host more meaningful women's ministry events?

While you may be tempted to skip ahead to the event and fellowship idea lists, I invite you to explore the purpose, types, format, and details of women's ministry fellowship.

It would be easy and convenient to flip through to the end of this book and randomly select ideas to plug into the fellowship gaps on your women's ministry calendar. Your group of women has unique, specific needs. Not every idea is the best idea for your women. We want our women to experience the best and so our team must strive to pray, plan, and prepare for the best events and fellowship opportunities.

What differentiates an event idea as good, better, and best? What a great question to discuss with your women's ministry team! In discussing this, you may want to consider:

- Does it support your ministry mission statement?
- What biblical truth women will remember?
- How do the preparations (décor, favors, teaching, devotionals) point women to Jesus, God, and the Word?
- Does it reflect fellowship as modeled in God's Word?

Your women's ministry mission statement should guide your fellowship selections. Our "why" provides a measuring stick to hold up against each idea; if the idea doesn't support our why, it needs to be tweaked or gently discarded. When we establish our why, it's much easier to complete the how. No worries, in this book, we'll cover both - the why and the how.

MY PRAYER FOR YOU

Lord, please help us to host more meaningful women's ministry events. Help us to know what types of fellowships, events, and activities our women need so they can become more like Christ. We want our women to grow in godliness, and we ask you to help us plan activities that encourage spiritual growth. Give us wisdom and inspiration to reach every woman in our church. Please guide us and bless our efforts. Amen.

CHAPTER 1

DEFINING FELLOWSHIP

WHAT IS FELLOWSHIP?

The online Merriam-Webster Dictionary defines fellowship as:

1. Companionship, company.
2. Community of interest, activity, feeling, or experience.
3. A company of equals or friends: association.[1]

Likewise, Christian fellowship can also be described as companionship, a community of interest, and a company of friends. Yet, Christian fellowship *should* be noticeably different. Your women's ministry fellowship shouldn't be mistaken for a birthday party, baby shower, or game-day cookout. Worldly fellowship and Christian fellowship should differ in décor and content. "Those who believe the gospel are united in the Spirit through Christ to the Father, and that unity is the basis of fellowship."[2] Christ sits at the center of Christian fellowship.

Our faith is what unites us no matter what season of life we're in, what type of job we have (or don't have), regardless of our marital status or our age. We are sisters in the family of Christ and our gatherings should reflect such. When we focus on the bond that unites us our connection grows stronger. Ecclesiastes 4:9-12 reminds us,

> "Two are better than one, because they have a good reward for their toil. For if they fall, one will lift up his fellow. But woe to him who is alone when he falls and has not another to lift him up! Again, if two lie together, they keep warm, but how can one keep warm alone? And though a man might prevail against one who is alone, two will withstand him—a threefold cord is not quickly broken."

We are better together.

We might assume every women's ministry event we host carries the marks of a Christian fellowship. As good Christian hostesses, we begin and end with a prayer and include a short devotional. Besides, all the women in attendance know and love Christ, right? Isn't that all that's needed? Maybe, but what if God's design for fellowship is a bit more focused? What if we saturated our events with our faith instead of just sprinkling on a little bit of Jesus?

I challenge you to prayerfully consider how a few tweaks might increase the impact of your fellowship, events, and activities. In most cases, they don't need an overhaul, they just need a bit of rethinking.

On the pages that follow you'll find specific ideas and scripture passages to help you and your team host more meaningful women's ministry events. You'll learn to select the best fellowship format, décor, door prizes, and devotionals that point women to Christ.

WHAT DOES THE BIBLE SAY?

What does the Bible say about fellowship? Pulling out my Strong's Concordance, I discovered some interesting information about fellowship. The Greek word for fellowship, *koinonia,* is used 12 times in the Bible. Definitions for *koinonia* include participation and common experiences and interests, recognized and enjoyed.[3] While similar to how the world defines fellowship, our common biblical beliefs are key to Christian fellowship.

Scripture describes fellowship as:

1. Partnership in the gospel (Philippians 1:5)
2. Relationship with the Father and with his Son Jesus Christ (1 John 1:3)
3. Relationship with the Holy Spirit (2 Corinthians 13:14)
4. Gathering of believers (Acts 2:42)

Fellowship is about relationship. Relationship with the Father, Jesus, the Holy Spirit, and other believers. I read through each occurrence of *koinonia* looking for an example of biblical fellowship in the local church. The gathering of believers in Acts 2:42 aligns most closely with fellowship opportunities the church, and women's ministry programs, offer today.

Before we examine Acts 2:42, let's look at the context of this passage. Acts 2 takes place on the day of Pentecost where all the believers were gathered in one place. "They were all filled with the Holy Spirit and began to speak in other tongues as the Spirit gave them utterance." (Acts 2:4) Everyone could "hear them telling in our own tongues the mighty works of God." (Acts 2:11b). Peter powerfully preaches a sermon using the scriptures to remind the crowd that the prophet Joel said these things would happen and that David foresaw and spoke about the resurrection of Christ. The people were convicted (v 36) and asked Peter what they must do (v 37). Peter responded, "Repent and be baptized every one of you in the name of Jesus Christ for the forgiveness of your sins, and you will receive the gift of the Holy Spirit." (v 38) As a result, over 3,000 accepted the message and were baptized.

Acts 2:42-47, says,

> "And they devoted themselves to the apostles' teaching and the fellowship, to the breaking of bread and the prayers. And awe came upon every soul, and many wonders and signs were being done through the apostles. And all who believed were together and had all things in common. And they were selling their possessions and belongings and distributing the proceeds to all, as any had need. And day by day, attending the temple together and breaking bread in their homes, they received their food with glad and generous hearts, praising God and having favor with all the people. And the Lord added to their number day by day those who were being saved."

Every day Christ-followers devoted themselves to meeting in the temple *and* they broke bread in their homes with joyful and humble hearts. The Lord added to them those who were being saved. They gathered every day as a response to hearing God's Word. It wasn't the physical food, the décor, or the people in attendance that drew them in; it was the Word of God and the testimony of other believers. The outpouring of the Holy Spirit resulted in a transformed community of believers. How God must desire we also live life as transformed believers in community.

A simple pattern emerged as God's people grew in number.

People turning to Christ → Shared worship and meals → shared possessions → shared worship and meals → people turned to Christ.[4]

Bible scholars refer to these gatherings of worship and meals as "table fellowship". Table fellowship included "music or other entertainment, but also discussion and even lectures... the topic of discussion recommended by Jewish priests was Scripture."[5] The fellowship of early Christians centered on worship, sharing, and learning the scriptures. By the 2nd century, pagan values overwhelmed the church and these intimate, scripture-centered, regular times of fellowship began to fade.[6] The slow fade of faith-focused fellowship began long ago. It's no wonder our church fellowship events don't often resemble those of the early Christian church.

Acts is not the only place we find this faith-focused model for fellowship. Jesus established this model for fellowship while He was on the earth, too. In John 13:1-20, we find Jesus and the disciples dining together. Jesus "rose from supper. He laid aside his outer garments, and taking a towel, tied it around his waist. Then he poured water into a basin and began to wash the disciples' feet and to wipe them with the towel that was wrapped around him." (John 13:3-5) Always teaching, Jesus wanted the disciples to experience and understand the lesson in verses 14-16. "If I then, your Lord and Teacher, have washed your feet, you also ought to wash one another's feet. For I have given you an example, that you also should do just as I have done to you. Truly, truly, I say to you, a servant is not greater than his master, nor is a messenger greater than the one who sent him." As you look through the four gospels, you'll find additional examples of fellowship with Jesus. It was never about the food; it was always about their faith.

The goal of fellowship in the early church was discipleship. In his reading of Acts 2, Warren Wiersbe notes "the three thousand new converts needed instruction in the Word and fellowship with God's people if they were going to grow and become effective witnesses."[7]

Wiersbe points out the early church included four critical elements of discipleship:

1. In depth teaching about their faith
2. Corporate fellowship with other believers

3. Participation in the Lord's supper
4. Active prayer[8]

Do we not have these same needs today? How should this affect our women's ministry fellowship offerings? Do we need to rethink our fellowship format so it also encourages discipleship?

Scripture is clear: fellowship among believers should encourage fellowship with Christ.

As we saw in Acts 2 and John 13, fellowship in New Testament times was:

- Gospel focused
- Action oriented

FELLOWSHIP AMONG BELIEVERS SHOULD ENCOURAGE FELLOWSHIP WITH CHRIST.

Participation was expected and encouraged. Those in attendance didn't gather only to eat, they received food *and* a biblical message. There was usually worship, entertainment, and an opportunity to serve others. How do we practically translate this into the fellowship events we host?

Hosting tips that infuse the gospel in our fellowship:

- Pray at the opening and closing
- Include time for women to pray in small groups
- Encourage women to read God's Word as a teaching anchored in scripture is shared
- Invite women to share personal stories of God's faithfulness
- Include a time for corporate worship – sing together
- Highlight God's Word – out loud, in the decor, in take-home favors, in event publicity
- Offer a service opportunity – service project, donation drive

- Seek to glorify God in everything you do and in every facet of the event

Can you see how a few changes or additions to your Soup and Salad Potluck could strengthen and encourage the faith of your women? Those additions and interactions have the potential to knit your women together, deepening their relationships and connections to one another. There's no mistake some translations (CEV for one) use the words "like family to each other" instead of the word fellowship. There's a difference in how we host family members, friends, and acquaintances. The level of formality decreases with familiarity. I spend less time cleaning and fussing when it's my family. While neither group probably cares about the dust bunnies hiding beneath my dining room furniture, those who grew up with me know I'm not a great housekeeper and there's no sense in pretending otherwise. I'm able to let my guard down a bit more with my family. The women in your church long to be treated like family. Your vulnerability allows them to be vulnerable. Your efforts to make them comfortable do not go unnoticed. I pray our sisters in Christ will see a difference in the way we host events for them.

CHAPTER 2

WHAT'S AT STAKE?

DESPITE THE BEAUTIFUL SISTERHOOD WE MAY HAVE ALREADY created, women's ministry is often viewed as an expendable, rather than meaningful, ministry within the church. When budgets need to be cut or church calendars are streamlined, ministries and activities that don't support the church's mission can wind up on the chopping block. While relationships are important, leaders ask, does this ministry or event help people know the Bible better? Does it help them to live out biblical truth?

The stats are stacked against us. Churches as a whole are struggling to impact the hearts and actions of believers. Studies have shown that believers have lost sight of a biblical worldview. What do I mean by that?

> "A biblical worldview [is] defined as believing that absolute moral truths exist; that such truth is defined by the Bible; and firm belief in six specific religious views... Jesus Christ lived a sinless life; God is the all-powerful and all-knowing Creator of the universe and He stills rules it today; salvation is a gift from God and cannot be earned; Satan is real; a Christian has a responsibility to share their faith in Christ with other people; and the Bible is accurate in all of its teachings."[9]

Research has shown "only 9% of self-identified Christians have a biblical worldview."[10] What does it mean if potentially nine out of every ten women attending your women's ministry fellowship do not have a biblical worldview? Regular Bible study and Sunday morning sermons have not been effective in cultivating a solid foundation of biblical truth. Many, if not most, of our women are unable to defend their faith. The faith of our women is fragile. Society is crumbling around us and our response in many cases has been to host potlucks and game nights with barely a hint of Jesus and a 5-minute devotional read out of a book. In many ways, the church in general has failed to equip women to stand firm in their faith. Christian fellowship events offer an opportunity for us to fortify their faith.

Feasting on a ministry menu filled with fellowship and food has altered the palate of many of our women. Many of us have trained the spiritual palates of our women to crave overly themed, heavily decorated, fellowship-focused events instead of hungering for Truth, theological discussions, and Christ-centered conversations. Your task may be to rewire their taste buds to crave fellowship with Christ.

What an impact we could make if every time we gathered, we remind our women:

- Who God is
- What Jesus has done for them (gave His life so they can live)

What if Jesus was never an afterthought or an addition, but Jesus was everything?

We began our journey examining Acts 2. If we follow the lives of the disciples in Acts 3 and 4, we learn John and Peter are jailed for teaching in the temple and healing the lame man. The officials told them to never again teach anything about Jesus. Peter and John did not bow to their demands. They replied, "We cannot keep quiet about what we have seen and heard." (Acts 4:20 CEV)

My prayer is that we will not keep quiet about what we have seen and what we have heard. We know who will reign victorious! We know the end of the story! We know where to find hope and freedom. Our women want to know these things too. Let's tell them!

CHAPTER 3

RETHINKING YOUR FELLOWSHIP FOCUS

PERHAPS YOU INHERITED A WOMEN'S MINISTRY CALENDAR THAT has been replicated year after year after year with only the slightest of tweaks. While there's nothing wrong with staying the course *if* it's working and *if* you're reaching every age group in your church, changing out just one event idea for something new can breathe fresh life into your women's ministry program. You may find doing something different allows you to reach women outside of the group of regular attendees.

Or, you may be a new leader that's been handed a blank ministry calendar and is feeling completely overwhelmed by all the options. There are so many things we *could* do, how do we decide *what* to do? You'd love a solution for the decision fatigue you're facing.

Whether your calendar needs something new or your team needs a master plan, the five types of fellowship listed below will help you develop a calendar filled with meaningful events that serve your women well while pointing them to Christ.[11]

Five Types of Fellowship

1. Holy Habits (also known as spiritual disciplines)
2. Biblical Encouragement
3. Practical Skills

4. Service
5. Connection

The goal is not to equally distribute two from each category on our women's ministry calendar but to offer a variety as the Lord leads. God may lead your team to emphasize service for the next year so every other month your ministry calendar includes a service opportunity. You might offer something that covers two or more categories at once, such as a Bible Journaling Workshop (holy habits and a practical skill).

Variety matters in ministry. Different types of women's ministry events will appeal to different women. For example, each time we offer a service project we see a shift in our attendance. Typically younger women outnumber the older women in attendance. A variety of events also keeps your program from becoming monotonous or stale. Shake things up a bit! Mixing up your events allows for lighter and deeper offerings to meet all levels of spiritual needs. Varying the focus of your women's ministry fellowship and events is key to a healthy and meaningful women's ministry program.

HOLY HABITS

Throughout the four gospels we see Jesus teaching and modeling holy habits for the disciples. Jesus was focused on their spiritual growth so they would be ready to "go therefore and make disciples of all nations, baptizing them in the name of the Father and of the Son and of the Holy Spirit, teaching them to observe all that I have commanded you." (Matthew 28:19-20a)

We have been given that same command to go and make disciples. We, too, need training to develop holy habits. Hosting events and activities that focus on holy habits allow women to learn, experience, and practice habits that lead to spiritual growth. Think of the habits the disciples practiced: studying the scriptures, prayer, worship, discernment, meditation, fasting, and evangelism.

Imagine the spiritual growth you could inspire in your women by offering in-depth teaching to sharpen a spiritual discipline. When you plan these events and activities, be sure you provide an opportunity for your women to apply and practice what they have learned. Don't just tell them about prayer, invite them to practice praying out loud at their tables. Just like fellowship in the early church, women want to be active, engaged, and participate. They want to *do* the thing you've been talking about.

For example, your team may see the need for building confidence in your women's ability to pray out loud. God used a very awkward moment during a summer Bible study session to move our team into action. Not one of the 21 women in attendance volunteered to close our time in prayer, many of whom had attended church for most of their lives. It was clear a little training was needed. On a Saturday morning, I led a Prayer Warrior Boot Camp which taught our women how to pray using the ACTS prayer method (adoration, confession, thanksgiving, supplication). We stretched and strengthened our prayer muscles as we practiced praying out loud with the women at our table. Our women returned home that morning with a tool they could use to help them pray out loud. We had great reviews from the women in attendance!

MEETING IDEAS

Bible journaling, prayer, how to study the Bible, how to honor the Sabbath, worship and prayer night, and how to share the gospel.

BIBLICAL ENCOURAGEMENT

When I think of biblical encouragement I think of Mary, Mother of Jesus, and her cousin, Elizabeth in Luke 1. Mary spent several days, if not months, with Elizabeth waiting for Jesus' birth. I imagine the time they spent together was filled with encouragement and reflecting on God's promises and faithfulness.

We can encourage our women with a teaching or testimony that highlights God's Word, faithfulness, and presence. Our encouragement must come from Christ and point women to Christ. God must be central to the message, and the application of biblical truth should always be encouraged.

Chapter 8, Rethinking Devotionals, is filled with tips for sharing testimonies.

Saturday Prayer Breakfasts are one way our team has hosted testimony-focused events. Women enjoyed a potluck or catered breakfast with a 20-minute testimony from a woman in our church, followed by a time of discussion or prayer at their tables. At a recent Prayer Breakfast, one of our pastor's wives shared what the Lord had been teaching her. Hearing her personal story of growing spiritually through multiple miscarriages touched the hearts of our women and encouraged them to look to the Lord in difficult seasons.

> **MEETING IDEAS**
>
> Guest speakers, personal testimonies,
> speaker panels, and topical teaching.

PRACTICAL SKILLS

Titus 2:3-5 encourages older women to teach younger women

many things, including practical skills such as caring for their home. Events and activities focused on practical skills allow women to learn, experience, and practice a valuable skill.

What is something your women want to learn how to do? Crochet? Make a pie crust? Use Instagram? Put Titus 2 into practice by utilizing the women in your church to teach these skills.

Whenever possible, the content should be framed through the lens of the Bible. An easy way to add the gospel to a skill-based meeting is to have a woman share a testimony that ties in with the topic. For example, someone might have a relative who taught them to knit, but also encouraged their faith. Another way to link the Bible to a skill-based meeting is to have a short lesson on what the Bible says about the topic. What does the Bible say about budgeting? What does the Bible say about being a good steward?

We've gotten away from the days when grandmothers and mothers taught their daughters how to cook, clean, iron, knit, sew, and can. The opportunity to learn those skills is appealing to women inside and outside of the church. An invitation to learn how to preserve strawberry jam may interest an unchurched neighbor who otherwise may have little interest in more spiritual church events. These types of events can be a great opportunity to reach women outside of the church.

A Workshop Night is an example of a practical skills event our team planned. Registration was necessary so money could be collected and supplies could be purchased. Attendees were able to choose between two activities: canvas painting and making homemade jam. One of our team members led the group that made jam. I opted for the painting workshop. A local artist led us in painting daffodils on a small canvas. Both groups enjoyed the opportunity to learn a new skill. The conversation while we worked was enjoyable too!

MEETING IDEAS

Painting parties, organizing, fashion tips, flower arranging, chalk paint, budgeting, canning, making jam, making pies, marriage workshops, meal planning, and discipline workshops.

SERVICE

Acts 2:44-45 highlights the early church's service to one another. "All who believed were together and had all things in common. And they were selling their possessions and belongings and distributing the proceeds to all, as any had need." Their love for one another and Christ led them to care for those in need in their community.

Each time our women's ministry team has offered a service opportunity, I've been thrilled to see women who don't attend any other women's ministry events show up. God always stirs the hearts of those in attendance for the needs of others. The fellowship that happens as we serve side-by-side leads to new and deeper friendships, as there's something about serving together that creates new bonds between believers.

My preference for a service fellowship is to invite a ministry partner to speak to our group (about 20-30 minutes) and use the rest of the time to complete a hands-on project to support that ministry.

Let me give you a quick example. We partnered with a local parachurch ministry that serves the homeless in our community. One of the program directors shared a very interesting and heart-breaking true story about one of their clients. Our women learned about the incredible impact that ministry can make in the lives of the homeless living in our community. Afterward, we assembled blessing bags for the homeless. We invited our women to take at least one to store in their car, so when they encountered a person in our community requesting food or money, they had a gift they could give to them. Side note: Next time I'd include a printed resource sheet with information on local food banks and shelters.

Introducing your women to local ministries allows women to discover ministries they may want to serve in regularly.

MEETING IDEAS

Prepare sandwiches for the homeless, create no-sew fleece blankets for the women's shelter, sew pillowcase dresses to send with a missionary, write note cards for local teachers, and cupcakes for emergency responders. You'll find additional service ideas at the end of the book.

CONNECTION EVENTS

We see countless examples of connection and relationship throughout the Bible. Jesus spends time not only with the disciples, but the sick and the sinners. How we interact with other people matters. Jesus instructs us to love one another *so that* everyone will know we are his disciples (John 13:34). The strength of our connections can point people to Christ.

The primary purpose of connection events is bringing people together to enjoy a communal activity, often a meal or a game. Attendees connect and deepen relationships with each other during the meal or while playing the game. Usually there is minimal structure (conversation is organic) and minimal planning required. Connection events can be very popular based on attendance, so-much-so it may be tempting to offer more connection events than other types of meetings.

Providing opportunities for our women to connect is important, but if we fill our calendars *only* with connection events, we do our women a disservice. Women's ministry must be about more than relationships with each other, it must *also* be about a relationship with Christ. Offering too many connection events could very easily water down your mission to share Christ and spur spiritual growth in your women. Remember, nine out of ten of the women at our events do not hold a biblical worldview. To maximize the impact of our women's ministry, connection events should be sprinkled lightly throughout the schedule, rather than applied liberally.

When hosting connection events, find ways to point women to the gospel. Sharing a testimony is an easy way to encourage women at these events to remind them of the hope and freedom found in Christ. You could also include Christ-focused door prizes to encourage spiritual growth (see chapter 7 for specific ideas).

Connection events are great for outreach events, too. They serve as a great bridge for women to attend other ministry events that you offer. Be sure to invite the women in attendance to Bible study and your next event. Once they experience the love of your women and hear about the love Christ has for them, no doubt they'll want to return again soon!

Game Nights have been a popular connection event with our women. They love to play board games, especially when we're away on our fall retreat. We hosted an evening game night where women could learn to play a card game (we played golf) or Catchphrase. After a time of snacks, an icebreaker game to give away some door prizes, and a brief word by our women's ministry director, we divided into groups and played games for the rest of the evening. If we do it again, we've discussed adding a 5-10 minute testimony.

Unlike the other four types of gatherings, connection events don't always require a date on the church calendar and the oversight of your women's ministry team. Chances are your women are already gathering in smaller groups, let's encourage more connections! Organic fellowship – the gathering of women in our church beyond our scheduled women's ministry events and activities – is something we can encourage and support.

MEETING IDEAS

Game nights, dinners, potlucks, holiday celebrations, fashion shows, and movie nights.

It's quite possible that your meeting may not fit neatly into one of the categories I've mentioned. Maybe it's a combination, and that's okay. That can be a good thing! Remember, the goal is not to offer one of each type of meeting every quarter or even every other month. We're not striving for an equal balance of different women's ministry meeting types; we are striving for a variety. Categorizing our meetings helps us to see the big picture and highlights any gaps in our programming.

As you make plans, keep in mind hosting regularly scheduled events and activities provides opportunities for women to connect and develop deeper relationships. If you can, strive to offer women's ministry meetings, fellowship, and events at least five to six times per year. Women need time to connect and develop deeper relationships. While your team may desire monthly ministry meetings or fellowship, I encourage you to honor the limitations that may have been placed on your team by your church staff.

Warren Wiersbe notes, "The Christians you meet in the

book of Acts were not content to meet once a week for 'services as usual.' They met daily (Acts 2:46), cared daily (Acts 6:1), won souls daily (Acts 2:47), searched the Scripture daily (Acts 17:11), and increased in number daily (Acts 16:5)."[12] May we not be content with meeting once a week for worship service and only a few times a year for women's ministry events.

I pray that offering a variety of women's ministry events and activities will impact both the spiritual growth of your women and increase their attendance.

CHAPTER 4

RETHINKING THE AGENDA FOR YOUR FELLOWSHIP

THE AGENDA OR FORMAT FOR WOMEN'S MINISTRY FELLOWSHIP, meetings, and events are going to look slightly different in every church, but each one should include some key components.

Before we establish WHAT our meeting will include, we need to establish WHY we're even meeting. Defining our why will help keep our women's ministry plans focused on God's specific plans for our women's ministry. I think we often get this process backwards. We hear a great idea, and then we figure out a way to make it fit our why. Go to God before you Google .

Use your why statement to determine a goal for the women who will be attending.

For example:

Why are we meeting? We've noticed many of our women do not want to pray out loud. Our meeting will teach women an easy method to pray out loud.

Goal: After our meeting, women will be able to use the ACTS prayer method to confidently pray out loud.

Once you've defined your goal for your fellowship or event, it will be much easier to assemble your agenda.

As we saw in Acts 2:42, early church fellowship gatherings include four core pieces:

1. Teaching
2. Fellowship
3. Breaking of bread
4. Prayer

Let's flesh these out and add a few practical items that will benefit those in attendance no matter your topic or focus.

FELLOWSHIP FRAMEWORK

1. Prayer - At minimum, include an opening and a closing prayer.
2. Announcements - Share upcoming opportunities for your women to grow, serve, and connect. Let them know what's next on your women's ministry calendar and how they can plug in and sign up.
3. Icebreaker - Icebreakers provide an opportunity for women to connect, to develop deeper relationships, and interact with the women in the room they may not know very well.
4. Testimony/Devotional - We need our women to share personal stories about what God is teaching them or doing in their lives.
5. Teaching - The teaching could be related to the theme or spiritual focus, or this could include activity directions.
6. Interaction - Through a planned activity such as a craft, a service project, or a workshop, or through small discussion groups providing opportunities for women to interact with one another versus only sitting and listening.

But what about a designated time for fellowship or connection? Organized icebreakers, discussion time after a teaching session, or even just chatting while completing a service project, *all* provide opportunities for connection. Adding a defined time for fellowship takes time away from other things on your agenda. Open fellowship time can also be incredibly uncomfortable for any new women in the room as those who know each other will quickly circle-up, leaving out those they don't know. While it can be tempting to leave the first 15 minutes open for socializing, you're inadvertently training your women to arrive late.

I enjoy time to catch up with friends I might not see except across the worship center and some of your women may feel the same. Women who desire additional connection time can be encouraged to socialize before and after your meetings. Parking lot conversations can be sweet and special too.

Women notice when we take the time to carefully plan out our events and fellowship. It shows that we value their time and we want them to have a great experience. Creating a framework for your events, fellowship, and activities will ensure your team keeps the focus on Christ.

CHAPTER 5

RETHINKING MISSIONS, SERVICE PROJECTS, AND OUTREACH EVENTS

THE EARLY CHURCH WAS KNOWN FOR HER GENEROSITY. IN ADdition to the biblical records, historians recorded the frustration of unbelievers that the generosity of Christians impacted the spread of Christianity.[13] Acts 2:42 says, "And they were selling their possessions and belongings and distributing the proceeds to all, as any had need. " Can the same be said of your women's ministry? Do others view your ministry as generous and regularly serving others? When I'm training women's ministry leaders, service is the one area leaders most often overlook.

The terms missions, service projects, and outreach are sometimes used interchangeably. The end goal is the same – sharing the love and message of Jesus with people outside of our church community, but their target, activity location, and purpose of each one vary.

You'll find a helpful chart on the following page.

	TARGET	WHERE?	WHY?
MISSIONS	Unbelievers	Foreign country or an area with few believers	To share the gospel
SERVICE PROJECTS	People in need; may or may not be a believer	Usually local; could occur off-site; could require delivery of items/needs	To provide a needed resource such as food, blankets, diapers, etc.
OUTREACH	Unbelievers	In the local community; could be an event hosted at the church	Share and show the love of Jesus; share the gospel; issue invitations to attend church services.

While your women's ministry program may pray for and support missions and outreach, your women's ministry program is most likely to participate in service projects. In addition to hosting your own opportunities to serve, encourage your women to serve with other ministry groups in your church too.

Don't overlook the ease of adding a service component to a women's ministry event. For example, ask women to bring a canned good, scarf, pack of diapers, or a gently-used coat to your next meeting.

Quick wins like gathering donations shines a light on ministries in your community women may be unaware of. Inviting women to bring a donation allows those with limited free time to participate. Ministries almost always have a need for physical supplies. Collecting donations helps those ministries meet immediate and critical needs.

If you can, include women outside of your team to take part in the delivery of the food, meal, or donations. Your team should not be the only ones participating in the blessing!

While one-and-done projects are usually quick and easy,

don't overlook the value of ministry partnerships. Sometimes God calls us to partner with just one ministry – to pour into them and to build relationships. God forever changed our women's ministry program in Kentucky when God led us to build a relationship with a local women's shelter. The eyes of our women were opened to needs in our community and the hearts of our women softened and grew as they loved and served the women at the shelter.

A few words of caution:

- Take care that the way you collect donations allows for women in all financial positions to participate. No uncomfortable basket passing. Please. Be grateful for donations of every size.
- Make sure your pastoral staff approves the project. Gracefully accept their recommendations and direction.

Look for ways you can incorporate service projects in your upcoming women's ministry events and fellowship. You'll find additional ideas in the back of the book.

OUTREACH ACTIVITIES

Like the gatherings of the early church, our fellowship and events should lead to an increase in the numbers of believers. Guests should be welcome and encouraged to attend future women's ministry fellowship and events. While our love for one another and the love we have for God has the potential to pique their curiosity about Christ, we do a great disservice if we don't tell those in attendance about Him. Some leaders worry that pushing Jesus could push guests away so they barely mention God.

Romans 10:14 makes it clear that we cannot expect people to believe without hearing the Word of God. "How can people have faith in the Lord and ask him to save them, if they have never heard about him? And how can they hear, unless someone tells them?" (CEV) What a gift and opportunity we have to tell people about the God who loves us and saved us from an eternity separated from Him! They won't be caught off guard; after all, they've been invited to a church event!

Fellowship with God is only accessible to followers of Christ. The goal of our fellowship should be to move women from desiring fellowship with friends to *also* desiring fellowship with Christ. 1 John 1:6-7 says, "If we say, 'We have fellowship with Him, yet we 'walk in darkness', we are lying and are not practicing the truth. But if we walk in the light as He Himself is in the light, we have fellowship with one another, and the blood of Jesus His Son cleanses us from all sin.'" If God is who we say He is, if He is Lord of our life, would we not tell others and invite them to experience the freedom and peace that God has given us?

CHAPTER 6

RETHINKING EVENT THEMES

I TAUGHT FIRST GRADE FOR FOUR YEARS BEFORE STAYING HOME with our boys. I was the queen of themes. I found ways to tie all the basic skills and curriculum requirements (math, reading, writing, science, and social studies) to any given topic. The décor in my classroom and well-crafted lesson plans used animals, plants, and more to deliver the content in a fun and creative way.

Some women's ministry teams have adapted a similar approach to their women's ministry events. The food, décor, devotional, and games all center around one concept or idea. Done with restraint and a focus on God's Word, themed events can help women remember the biblical truth and focus of their time together. Sometimes, though, events look more like a first-grade classroom studying bears than a church event for Christian women.

Women's ministry themes aren't all bad. Your leader or team may have prayed for a scripture verse or passage to use as focus or thread connecting the women's ministry events and activities for the year. Repeatedly pointing women to a biblical truth and dedicating time to studying and applying that truth will build biblical literacy as women study that passage in scripture. As the theme creates a thread of connection between events women can know and understand God's Word in new ways.

I've spent a lot of time pondering how historical women's ministry transitioned from the Acts 2 early church to a missions focus in the late 1800's to the fellowship focus we see in many churches today. Pinterest, social media, and the internet highlight the visual aspects of our women's ministry events. Images we see as we search for women's ministry ideas focus on tablescapes, beautiful buffets, photo booths, and stage décor. Rarely do we, or can we, see the biblical lessons taught and learned at women's ministry fellowship, events, and activities.

We've been duped into thinking women's ministry events should be and are supposed to be visually appealing. We've used cutesy themes, décor, and teachings, many of which look like they've been pulled from Sunday school lesson plans for elementary-age children or a Vacation Bible School curriculum. Women want and need age-appropriate teachings that build their Bible knowledge. Certainly, there's nothing wrong with pretty things and decorative touches, but it's worth assessing if our décor dominates, rather than supports, the purpose of our gathering. Women need meaningful meetings, not just pretty parties.

EVENT NAMES

What we name our events sets expectations and influences our impact too.

- Cute or cheesy names (Jesus Loves You Berry Much or Shecuterie) create confusion where you need clarity. Women have no idea if they'll benefit from attending.
- Fun names reinforce the belief that women don't desire sound biblical teaching and topics.
- Rhyming and alliteration can repel the very women you want to attract.
- A fluffy or kitschy name (Chips, Dips, and Fellow-sips or

Soul Sisters) can signal your event is lacking in depth.

- Puns are outdated. It may have worked well in the 90's but they repel most younger women.
- Women aren't likely to take the event seriously if it borders on silly.

Before you label me a party pooper, let me explain. Event names should communicate the activity and purpose. Strive for clarity and reduce confusion. Women should know without a doubt the event is for them. Some teams use the same general name, (Ladies Connect, Girlfriends, Women's Gathering, Women's Fellowship) and add a descriptive subtitle (worship night, workshops, blessing bags, Bible study tips). Don't overcomplicate it. Keep things simple and the focus on Christ.

ATTRACTING ATTENDEES

The early church in Acts 2 was an active and growing church. What spurred their growth?

We see unbelievers were drawn by two things:

1. Christ-exalting praise
2. Christlike love[14]

This should come as no surprise. John 13:34-35 says, "A new commandment I give to you, that you love one another: just as I have loved you, you also are to love one another. By this all people will know that you are my disciples, if you have love for one another." People notice when we sacrificially care for fellow church members and those outside of the church. Christian historical writings document Christian generosity to the poor because it was so unique and unusual.[15] Compassion, not décor, prizes, or fancy food, attract people to Christ.

The early church didn't just *attract* unbelievers, they

converted unbelievers. "People were converted daily because be-lievers were evangelizing daily."[16] Early Christians didn't keep the good news to themselves, they shared it boldly and broadly. Their willingness to evangelize resulted in the Lord adding "to their number day by day those who were being saved." (Acts 2:47) The faith of the early Christian church was contagious! There would have been no mistaking their gatherings for a neighborhood potluck or baby shower. Even passersby would have noticed their Christlike love and Christ-exalting praise. Would a guest at your last women's ministry fellowship be able to say the same?

COMPASSION ATTRACTS PEOPLE TO CHRIST.

May God help us to highlight Him as we plan each detail of our events.

CHAPTER 7

RETHINKING DINNER, DÉCOR, AND DOOR PRIZES

DINNER

Most of my adult life I've been a member of a Southern Baptist Church (with a few God-ordained detours). Like peanut butter and jelly, food and fellowship went hand-in-hand. To host a women's ministry event and not offer some type of food was almost unheard of. We often operated under the belief that the greater the spread, the greater the turnout.

The early church in Acts 2 liked to eat, too! Acts 2:42 includes the "breaking of bread" in its description of gathering together. Scholars believe the breaking of bread can refer to the Lord's Supper (partaking of bread and wine in remembrance of Christ) and it can refer to having a meal together. Yet, faith not the food that was served was always the focus.

DÉCOR

You are likely blessed with women on your team and in your church that are incredibly gifted in the arts of hospitality and decorating. They can create elaborate tablescapes and transform your church gym rendering it unrecognizable. What a blessing they can be!

In Luke 10:38-42, Jesus has come to the home of sisters Mary and Martha. Instead of helping Martha serve their guests, Mary has placed herself at the feet of Jesus, much to Martha's dismay. When Martha complains to Jesus that her sister is not helping, Jesus responds, "there is only one thing worth being concerned about. Mary has discovered it, and it will not be taken away from her." (NLT) Jesus did not instruct Mary to continue with her hostessing duties, instead, He praised Mary for setting aside her duties to listen to His teaching. May this serve as a reminder that gathering our women at the feet of Jesus is our priority.

Content should always trump decor. Too much décor can be a distraction at your event. I've watched women lose interest in a speaker as they've been unable to see around tall centerpieces. Heavily decorated stages make it easy to lose focus on the message. A good hostess makes careful choices so as not to detract from the meaning of the gathering.

TAKE-HOME FAVORS

Roaming through the aisles of a local thrift store with a friend recently, I stopped suddenly when I saw the display of white bells highlighting various cities and states. Memories of collecting bells on our family vacations came rushing back. I no longer have my bell collection, but our Christmas tree is adorned with ornaments from family vacations. Flashes of special memories accompany the proper placement of each ornament, from the death-defying ride down the tornado at the Great Wolf Lodge to the pies from the Whistle Stop Café in Kentucky.

Mementos from women's ministry retreats and events have the same effect. A memory of a conversation with my roommate, an impactful story from our speaker, or just a wash of warmth as

I recall a cold fall weekend away with sisters in Christ.

What do you want your women to remember about your event? Take-home favors can be a token of remembrance that reminds your women of the spiritual truth they heard at your event. Or not. Do you want your women to remember the ice cream they ate or the scripture verse that was shared during the teaching time? Do you want your women to drink out of a coffee mug with a catchy event title or do you want them to see God's Word every time they take a sip of their morning coffee? What will stand out in their minds as they reflect on your fellowship? The décor or Christ?

I'm not saying we can't be creative, but does your creativity point women to Christ?

For Christ-focused favors place your event's focal scripture verse or phrase in/on:

- Pretty frames
- Bookmarks
- Coloring page
- Phone lock screen
- Mug
- Tote bag
- Jewelry
- T-shirt
- Pen
- Sticker
- Journal

Challenge your team to create décor and favors that lead your women to focus on God's Word for the days and weeks to come after your event. Give them the freedom and budget to create or purchase something that will drive home the biblical message.

If time allows, your women could craft their own take home

favor. At our next retreat we'll be making ribbon Bible book-marks. The cardstock we'll glue the ribbons on will have our theme "cultivate 2022" printed on them.

DOOR PRIZES

If your budget allows, favors and door prizes that point women towards Christ can be nice, but they're not necessary. And to be honest, very nice door prizes distract from the event and can be a source of jealousy among your women. I shop year-round for door prizes that cost $5 or less. I'm always on the lookout for great deals!

My very favorite way to give away door prizes at women's ministry events is a door prize basket. I fill a basket with lots of door prizes roughly the same value. When women are selected to receive a door prize, they get to choose the prize they want out of that door prize basket. The key is to have more prizes than the number of people you're going to give prizes to because no one wants the last thing that's left in the basket. (You feel like you're getting the leftovers.) It also ensures each door prize winner can pick something that they want or will use.

Door Prize Ideas

- Jewelry, like a necklace with a scripture verse on it
- Bracelet with a verse or an encouraging word
- Stationery sets, pens, sticky notes, all those kinds of fun things
- Framed scripture verses or plaques
- Insulated cups, tumblers, all those types of things (I love finding them with a verse on them.)
- Devotional books
- Personal Bible studies
- Christian movies (A lot of times, I'm able to find those for $5 or less.)

- Pretty note card sets or notepads
- $5 gift cards for coffee, frozen yogurt, or your local Chick-fil-A®
- Christian fiction books (Make sure you're choosing a book you know is solid.)

Door prizes are another way that we can be intentional about pointing our women to Christ. We can fill our door prize basket with meaningful mementos that will remind them who their Savior is and who they are in Christ.

CHAPTER 8

RETHINKING ICEBREAKER ACTIVITIES

WOMEN TYPICALLY HAVE A LOVE/HATE RELATIONSHIP WITH ICE-breaker games. They either love them, or they hate them. Past experiences with silly games, unenthusiastic game leaders, or lengthy games that steal the speaker's time can leave a sour taste in the mouths of women who would otherwise enjoy making new connections.

Yet, icebreaker games can be an effective tool to get to know women outside of our social circles and bust up the cliques that tend to dominate women's ministry events. Great icebreakers provide points of connection for your women through shared experiences and interests.

Things like:

- Who here doesn't like to eat chocolate?
- Find someone in the room who played an instrument in high school.
- Get the signature of someone who's been on a mission trip.
- Stand up if you start your day with coffee.

God can use icebreakers to make connections among the women at your event as they share details they might not otherwise. Whether it's the love of the same hobby, a shared travel destination, or a Christmas tradition, creating avenues for such details to be shared reveals hearts and journeys.

If you've used any of the games on the Women's Ministry Toolbox website, you may have noticed they're not very spiritual. That's on purpose. Jumping right into spiritual questions can feel much too personal. Spiritual questions can also put some of your women on the defensive, shutting down conversations before they get started. Icebreakers should prime the pump. Surface-level conversations now will encourage your women to go deeper later during your table discussion. You've broken the ice!

SPIRITUAL QUESTIONS AND BIBLE GAMES

I was at an event many years ago where we played several individual icebreaker games. The winners each received a very nice door prize (significantly more than the $5 limit I suggest). One particular game ruffled my feathers. We were given ten really hard, random trivia questions to answer. Two of them were Bible-based and the rest were not. If your Bible knowledge was lacking, you were immediately at a disadvantage.

I heard many of the women around me grumbling about how hard the questions were. They were next to impossible to answer. Instead of being fun, that icebreaker game was frustrating! If we had played in teams rather than individually, I think the response could have been much different.

Bible games are great for people who know the Bible. It is best to assume there are women in attendance who did not grow up in the church or do not have a strong biblical background.

Likewise, spiritual questions are best for table discussion after a teaching or speaker's session, and in closed small groups with established relationships where trust has already been built

–Bible study groups later in the semester, your women's ministry team, or table mates later in the retreat weekend.

ICEBREAKER TIPS

To encourage connection and fellowship consider:

- Keeping your prizes small ($5 or less) to eliminate jealousy.
- Steering clear of any controversial topics (breastfeeding, politics, homeschooling, etc.).
- Adapting instructions based on the physical limitations of your specific group. For example, raising your hand instead of standing up or asking them to keep score instead of actively participating.
- Dividing your women into random teams to break apart cliques. By color, numbers, or stickers on name tags.
- Providing the option to choose another question or skip an item. We never know what might cause discomfort or anxiety.
- Squelching any oversharing and stopping any sharing of secrets or lies.
- Playing trivia-type games in teams.
- Asking for volunteers for games in front of the group so no one feels embarrassed.

Unlike many Christians in the early church, most of our women aren't living life in community with each other. We don't run into each other while gathering water at the well. We're not meeting regularly in each other's homes for meals, prayer, teaching, and fellowship. While we may jump right into community with the few women we know well from Bible study or small groups, we may need a bit of a nudge and designated time to grow relationships with women outside of our social circle.

Icebreaker games can quicken those connections as women share and laugh together.

CHAPTER 9

RETHINKING DEVOTIONALS

IN MY FIRST FEW YEARS AS A WOMEN'S MINISTRY LEADER, I gathered sweet stories from books and online articles to share as devotionals during our women's ministry meetings. I wanted to encourage our women to look for Christ at work in their own lives. While I'm sure those stories made an impact, I realize now how much more meaningful it would have been to have our team and the women in our church share personal stories rather than reading the stories of celebrities or strangers.

Many leaders use the words devotional and testimony interchangeably, but I think there's a distinct difference. A testimony is often defined as the personal retelling of the moment of conversion. It's a story of an encounter with Christ or the moment of salvation. The Merriam-Webster online dictionary defines a religious testimony as a "public profession of religious experience."[17]

While a testimony is, and can be, about the singular point at which we accepted Christ as Savior, a testimony can also communicate any experience we've had with God. Devotionals, on the other hand, are written testimonies, usually written by an author or a Christian speaker. Did you catch that? Devotionals are *someone else's story, someone else's testimony.*

I know it's easier to share other people's stories than our own but, like grabbing a fast-food meal at a drive-thru, sharing a devotional we found online or in a book is convenient and it may feed our women, but it isn't what's best. When our women hear other women in the church share what God has done in their lives, it makes a greater impact than any devotional read out of a book ever could! Suddenly, it's personal. It's someone that we know! And your women begin to believe that maybe, just maybe, God can help them too. Sharing personal testimonies, instead of devotionals, connects the heart of our women, and it opens the door for Titus 2 relationships.

WHY?

Why should we share our testimonies? God makes it clear in his Word that all believers have a responsibility to tell others about Him.

1 Chronicles 16:8 says, "Give praise to the Lord, proclaim his name, make known among the nations, what he has done."

Romans 10:14 (NLT) says, "But how can they call on him to save them unless they believe in him? And how can they believe in him if they have never heard about him? And how can they hear about him unless someone tells them?"

1 Peter 3:15 says, "Always be prepared to give an answer to everyone who asks you to give the reason for the hope that you have."

We share testimonies to help women view life with an eternal perspective. We share testimonies to encourage one another, give hope, create connection, model obedience, and inspire our women to look for God's fingerprints on their current situations and circumstances. Testimonies provide a testimony of God's faithfulness and love. Testimonies open the door for the sharing of the gospel. There are times in which our women may not be able to feel or see God clearly, but hearing others reflect on God's faithfulness in difficult circumstances can be a huge encouragement.

HOW DO WE SHARE OUR TESTIMONIES?

I suggest we adopt new terminology. Let's use the word "stories" instead of "testimonies" – that word comes with a whole lot of pressure. A simple word swap can make a huge difference. Stories are familiar. They are comforting. All stories have a beginning, a middle, and an end, and our stories should be presented in a similar manner.

God has provided us with numerous examples throughout the Bible of people who encountered Him and their lives were changed. John 9 tells the story of Jesus giving sight to a blind man. When asked what had happened, the blind man replied, "The man they call Jesus made some mud and put it on my eyes. He told me to go to Siloam and wash. So I went and washed, and then I could see." (John 9:11)

While our testimony might not be as short as those three sentences, the format is one that we can apply to our stories as we share.

First, the story consists of three parts:

1. How I was
2. What happened
3. How I am now.

Second, the story focuses on what Jesus did.
And third, transformation is celebrated.
When you consider writing out your personal testimony or teaching your women to share their stories, remember these three Cs.

3 CS

1. Current – Focus on a recent lesson the Lord has taught you within the last year or two, if possible. Keeping it current reminds women God is always at work.
2. Concise – Remember, this is not a speaking or teaching session. What you share should last 5-10 minutes, no more. Practice sharing it. Record yourself and listen to it to make sure your story is coming across as intended. Make a few notes so you don't lose focus.
3. Christ-centered – Keep it focused on what God has done, not on the dramatic details. It's about Him. It's not about you. You want your women to remember what God accomplished through you or through the circumstances. When our eyes are focused on God, others see and learn by our example.

Here are a few more words of caution as you consider sharing your story.

- Please do not share anything that would embarrass someone or lead them to gossip.
- Protect your spouse, your family, and anyone who is a part of your story.
- When sharing with a group, we want to be more general than we do specific. Be prayerful and careful with the details.
- If possible, get permission and input from anyone who is a part of your story. If you're sharing about a hard season in your marriage, your spouse needs to be completely aware and on board with what you're sharing.

Use caution when asking women to share about their current issues or struggles. We want to remove any chance that their story might be driven by anger or bitterness. Stories of hope and healing can be incredibly powerful, but take care to keep the focus on spiritual transformation and God, rather than emotions and the flesh. Ask God for discernment as you review their written story. It might be better for them to share when they have journeyed a bit further down the road or healed a bit more.

SHARING THE GOSPEL

You may be wondering; do we always need to share the gospel and invite women to accept Christ as their Lord and Savior after a testimony has been shared?

Your church likely has processes and procedures for sharing the gospel, and your team may not feel that every women's ministry or activity warrants a verbal presentation of the gospel. However, I want to encourage you to include "the how" in some way, either verbally, written, or via invitation. You might want to provide a tract or a brochure that provides the steps for accepting Christ as Savior or invite women to speak to a prayer counselor or women's ministry team member.

If God truly is everything we claim He is, women want and expect an invitation. Don't let them leave your women's ministry event or activity without a path to "the how" – that night may be the very night God is calling them to submit to Him, to repent of their sin, and accept Him as Lord and Savior.

With a bit of intentional prayer and preparation, sharing our stories and sharing the gospel can become a regular and anticipated experience at your women's ministry fellowship, events, and activities. Let your team be the ones to go first, to model the sharing of their stories. It's going to inspire and encourage your women in ways you may not even begin to imagine. Every story has the power and the ability to point our women to Christ and to encourage them in their walk.

CHAPTER 10

BLESSINGS AND BENEFITS

As you can see, the blessings and benefits of rethinking fellowship are numerous. With just a few minor tweaks, we can take our events and ultimately our women's relationships with each other and Christ to the next level.

Looking back at fellowship in the early church reminds us our goal stretches beyond traditional hosting duties. Our most important task is to encourage and equip our women to grow in holiness. But we are also responsible for facilitating connections between women and pushing them beyond their social circle. One of the biggest complaints about women's ministry is that it's filled with cliques. While it's wonderful that our women love each other fiercely and they can be incredibly loyal, excluding others isn't kind or Christ-like. Helping our women to connect with others outside of their circle reflects the heart of Christ and His vision for the church.

When our offerings shift from focusing mostly on connection to cultivating spiritual growth our women, their families, and the church body benefit. Rethinking fellowship allows our team to move our women's ministry program from *merely* meeting to *meaningful* meetings. Saturating everything we do with Jesus invites women to do the same. Sharing stories of God's faithfulness at our events opens our women's eyes what He is doing in their lives. When women take the skills and confidence they've acquired at our women's ministry events, we see a difference in the way they pray, read their Bible, and share their faith. As culture continues to shift further from biblical truth, women's ministry will help our women stay anchored. May we be valued as an essential ministry in our local church.

The time has come for you to get to work. I challenge you to spend time as a team considering how you can increase the benefits and blessings of your women's ministry events, activities, and fellowships. How will you host meaningful women's ministry events? As you consider the hundreds of event ideas that follow, always be thinking about how your team can focus your women on Christ.

FELLOWSHIP IDEA LISTS

PLEASE NOTE: SOME IDEAS ARE LISTED IN MULTIPLE CATEGORIES. As you skim through each list, please pray and ask the Lord to reveal which ideas are best for your specific group of women.

- Christmas
- Crafts
- Entertainment
- Faith-focused
- Fall
- Food
- Fun & Games
- Interest Groups
- Outdoor
- Outreach
- Service Projects
- Sports
- Spring
- Summer
- What does the Bible say about _____ ?
- Winter
- Workshops

CHRISTMAS

Women's ministry teams tend to recycle the same Christmas event idea year after year. I want to encourage you to make it a matter of prayer before hitting the repeat button. Yes, it may be a popular event, but does God desire something different for your women this year?

Some ideas are listed in multiple categories.

Blessings and Serving Others

1. Assemble and send care packages to college students as they take their final exams or men and women serving overseas.
2. Buy coffee for people at a local coffee shop.
3. Christmas caroling – visiting specific church members and visitors, provide cookies and cocoa for a quick post caroling party
4. Christmas for missionaries – collect and wrap gifts/ write and send cards to missionaries for Christmas
5. Christmas for others – throw a party for your church staff, seniors, shelter, nursing home, etc.
6. Deck the Halls – decorate the yard/home of a special member or family (surprise a critically ill family with a Christmas display in their yard)
7. Deck the halls of the church – come together to decorate the church for Christmas – might include making new decorations.
8. Decorate Christmas cookies – distribute to homebound members, etc.
9. Help the families in your church who are fostering children with Christmas gifts.
10. Host a shoebox filling party for a local or international ministry.

11. Make Christmas cookies and deliver them to firefighters, police officers, or nurses at your local hospital
12. No-sew fleece blankets for the homeless
13. Random Acts of Kindness – send your group out to do RAOKs.
14. Serve the single moms in your church by offering childcare one evening so they can go Christmas shopping.
15. Simply Still – Night of worship, reflection, silence, and prayer
16. Spread some Christmas cheer with the Gift of No Dishes throughout a neighborhood near your church. Be sure to add an invite to your church's Christmas activities and a list of upcoming women's ministry events to each bag.
17. Throw a Christmas party for others – teachers, nurses, emergency responders, women in a shelter, your church staff.

Check Items off your Christmas List

1. Christmas card party – everyone brings their cards to address
2. Gift wrapping party – everyone brings their own gifts and paper
3. Christmas cookie exchange

Festive Food Ideas

1. Christmas candy making workshop
2. Christmas potluck/tasting party – everyone shares a favorite/new holiday dish
3. Cookie exchange

4. Decorate Christmas cookies – distribute to homebound members, etc.

Just for Fun

1. Birthday party for Jesus – bring gifts for local children, seniors, homebound, angel tree, etc.
2. Christmas bingo – play regular bingo, with the winners receiving $5 gifts
3. Christmas display viewing – provide map and directions to light displays around town
4. Christmas light scavenger hunt
5. Christmas movie viewing
6. Christmas scavenger hunt – outdoors or indoors
7. Gift exchange
8. My Favorite Things party - Attendees bring a favorite kitchen tool, beauty product, etc. under a $20 value for a gift exchange or for show-and-tell..
9. Ornament exchange
10. World Crafts – host a fair-trade shopping party.

Learn Something New/Crafty Ideas

1. Christmas around the world – pick a country(ies) where your church has missionary connections and learn about the food and customs
2. Christmas candy making workshop
3. Christmas craft workshops – offer at least two options for the crafts
4. Christmas Pinterest project party
5. Christmas traditions party – share family traditions
6. Christmas tree decorating demo – bring in an interior designer to give tips on how to make your tree looks its best

7. Gift making party – provide supplies for everyone to make homemade hot cocoa, cookies in a jar, homemade bath scrub, etc.
8. Gift wrapping demos – teach women various ways to wrap gifts
9. Ornament decorating party – set up stations and let folks rotate

CRAFTS

1. Beading/Jewelry Making
2. Blanket Making
3. Canvas Painting Class
4. Flower Arranging
5. Holiday Crafts
6. Knitting/Crochet
7. Mosaic Tiles
8. Ornament Making
9. Paint Your Own Pot
10. Pinterest Party
11. Scrapbooking
12. Sewing
13. UFO Night – Unfinished Object Night
14. Wreath Making

ENTERTAINMENT & THEATER

1. Ballet
2. Broadway Show
3. Christian Book Club
4. Christian Concert
5. Christian Movie Night
6. (Clean) Comedy Show/Club
7. Comedy Recording
8. Dinner Theater
9. Historical Tour
10. Museum Tour
11. Musical
12. Mystery Dinner
13. Orchestra Performance
14. Play
15. Special Holiday Show/Event

FAITH-FOCUSED

While every fellowship event we offer should have a faith-focus, some fellowship serves as a training ground. Encourage your women to grow spiritually by providing opportunities for them to practice spiritual disciplines. We can be intentional about growing and encouraging each woman's spiritual journey – and still have fun!

Don't be afraid to go deep – the key is leading women deeper into the content. Unchurched and new Christians need definitions, explanations, context, and summaries.

Also check out the "What does the Bible say about ___?" list.

1. Back-to-School prayer event
2. Bible journaling
3. Bible Study Boot Camp (see my READ Bible Study Kit for Groups listed in the resource section)
4. Bible study skills
5. Biblical hospitality
6. Brunch/Breakfast with Bibles (teaching or testimony is shared)
7. Care packages or cards for missionaries
8. Christian book club meetings
9. Discernment
10. Evangelism
11. Fasting
12. Learning to pray out loud (see my Prayer Warrior Boot Camp Kit)
13. Learning to use digital tools for Bible study
14. Missions banquet
15. Prayer breakfasts
16. Prayer night
17. Prayer stations

18. Prayer walks
19. Scripture memory workshop
20. Series on bible terms (salvation, sanctification, justification, baptism, worship, complementarian, egalitarian, etc.)
21. Series on the Fruit of the Spirit
22. Series on men and women of the faith
23. Series on missionaries
24. Sharing your faith stories workshop
25. Spiritual gifts assessment
26. Teaching a prayer or Bible study method (ACTS, READ, etc.)
27. Testimony sharing
28. Worship night

FALL

Fall offers some unique fellowship opportunities for your women.

- To fellowship outdoors.
- To gather and do all sorts of "fall" things.
- To experience the smells and tastes of fall.

I've subdivided these fall fellowship ideas into five categories: blessing others, crafty ideas, food ideas, head outdoors, and meet up.

Bless Others

1. Attend a high school football game and cheer for the Youth from your church. Make signs!
2. Bless families with pumpkins that might not otherwise purchase any.
3. Make and take Homeless Blessing Bags.
4. Plant bulbs at your church or a local school.
5. Put together no-sew fleece blankets for a local shelter.
6. Rake leaves at a homebound member's house.
7. Work together on a Fall Festival booth or Trunk or Treat display.

Crafty Ideas

1. Carve pumpkins together.
2. Host a fall craft night.
3. Make fall wreaths together.
4. Make scarves.

Food Ideas

1. Bake fall flavored cupcakes.

2. Dedicate an evening to desserts – featuring pies of all kinds.
3. Dip and decorate caramel apples.
4. Grab your crockpots and have a soup social.
5. Hold a chili contest.
6. Host a pumpkin flavor party! Ask everyone to bring an item to share.
7. Make and can applesauce or apple butter together.
8. Mix-up custom bags of trail mix – make extras to take to homebound members, church staff, or your local fire station.
9. Set up a progressive dinner.
10. Teach the group how to make an apple pie – homemade crust and all!

Head Outdoors

1. Attend a football game. Guys aren't the only ones who like sports!
2. Build a bonfire.
3. Drive up to an apple orchard.
4. Hike through the woods.
5. Host a s'mores making party. (Try them with Reese's cups!)
6. Make your way through a corn maze.
7. Pick out pumpkins at a patch.
8. Saddle up some horses and hit the riding trails.
9. Take a prayer walk on a nature trail.
10. Take a road trip to see the changing fall leaves.

Meet Up

1. Beat the rush and meet up for some early Christmas shopping.

2. Check out a local flea market.
3. Go to a museum.
4. Have a ladies night out at the local county fair.
5. Grab dinner – eat outside if it is not too chilly!
6. Host a Fantasy Football League for "girls only".
7. Meet at the movies.
8. Play Bunko.
9. Take a walking tour.

FOOD

1. Appetizers
2. "Blue" foods (or other food theme i.e. Italian, Mexican, etc.)
3. Breakfast foods
4. Candy making
5. Charcuterie boards (make or bring)
6. Chocolate tasting
7. Coffee shop
8. Cookie decorating
9. Cookie swap
10. Cooking class
11. Cooking competition
12. Cupcake decorating
13. Dessert
14. Dinner and recipe swap
15. Festival of Tables (hostesses decorate tables)
16. Freezer cooking
17. Ice cream tasting party
18. Make your own pizza
19. Picnic
20. Pie night
21. Potluck
22. Progressive dinner
23. Soup swap/tasting
24. Taco bar
25. Tea

FUN & GAMES

1. Accessory Swap
2. Antique Shopping
3. Bingo
4. Board Games
5. Book Swap
6. Bowling
7. Bunko
8. Card Games
9. Christmas Light Scavenger Hunt
10. Clothing Swap
11. Consignment Shopping
12. Holiday Party (Valentine's Day, St. Patrick's Day, etc.)
13. Historic District Shopping
14. Mall Scavenger Hunt
15. Outlet Shopping
16. Scavenger Hunt
17. Spa Night

INTEREST GROUPS

Interest groups allow women to connect through a shared interest. While most may not be faith-focused, you can infuse interest group meetings with faith by encouraging group leaders to begin and end with prayer, share a short personal testimony, and glorify God through godly conversations.

1. Abortion Recovery
2. Baking
3. Biking
4. Book Clubs
5. Cooking Club
6. Crafts
7. Divorce Care Group
8. Empty-Nesters
9. Fitness
10. Gardening
11. Grief Care Group
12. Hiking
13. Kayaking
14. Knitting & Crochet
15. Moms Group
16. Movie Group
17. Prayer Group
18. Recovery Group
19. Scrapbooking
20. Sewing
21. Single Moms
22. Supper Club
23. Tennis
24. Walking

OUTDOOR

1. Cave tour
2. Christian exercise class
3. Firepit
4. Gardening
5. Go-karts
6. Golf
7. Hiking
8. Horseback riding
9. Ice cream social
10. Ice skating
11. Kayaking
12. Nature walk
13. Paddle boarding
14. Picnic
15. Pilates
16. Pool party
17. Prayer walk
18. Putt-Putt
19. Roller skating
20. Self-defense class
21. Snow skiing
22. Snow tubing
23. Walking
24. Water park
25. Water skiing
26. Water tubing
27. Zumba

OUTREACH IDEAS

Outreach events typically draw unchurch women by offering a mostly secular evening. However, we should always include a faith-focus at each event.

1. Comedy show
2. Concert
3. Fashion show
4. Game night
5. Interest groups (see Interest Group list)
6. Movie night
7. Sporting event
8. Tourist excursion (historical home, nature site, boutique shopping)
9. Workshops (see Workshop list)

SERVICE PROJECTS

If you haven't read chapter 5 on Missions, Service Projects, and Outreach, please read that first.

Be sure to check with the Missions Team or Missions Pastor at your church to find out which parachurch ministries your church already has a partnership with. Prayerfully consider a long-term partnership with one ministry in your area so you can build relationships with the residents or recipients. Be sure to ask the ministry what needs they have – they may have an abundance of food pantry items, but need them to be organized.

I've divided service projects into four different categories.

- Cook, Craft, and Create
- Random Acts of Kindness
- Shop with Purpose
- Volunteer Your Time

May God guide your team to the project He desires for your group as you encourage women to live out their faith!

Craft, Cook, and Create

1. Assemble and distribute blessing bags for women who need some encouragement.
2. Bake goodies, such as cupcakes, and deliver them to your local police or fire station.
3. Cards for college students
4. Cards for homebound
5. Cards for those serving in the military
6. Cards for missionaries
7. Create a community garden.
8. Create birthday bags for your local food pantry (birthday cake, hats, candles, balloons)

9. Cut out shoes for Sole Hope.
10. Fill a freezer with meals for a new mom.
11. Gather together to assemble no-sew fleece blankets for a local children's home or women's shelter.
12. Host a sandwich making party and pass them out to the homeless.
13. Knit or crochet prayer shawls and lap blankets for church members and friends that are facing health challenges.
14. Pack shoeboxes for a local or international ministry.
15. Paint and decorate the teacher's lounge at a struggling school.
16. Provide a meal for families at your local Ronald McDonald House.
17. Put together and distribute homeless bags.
18. Put together Sonshine Boxes or bags and bless women in your church or community.
19. Rescue mission – serve a meal
20. Sew some pillowcase dresses for children in another country.
21. Take a meal to a widow, homebound member, single mom, or recent divorcee in your church or community.
22. Write letters or send cards to missionaries.

Donate and Shop with a Purpose

1. Bless a children's hospital with fun Band-Aids.
2. Collect gently used clothes and donate them to a ministry in need.
3. Donate children's books and movies to a local children's hospital.
4. Donate food to a local food shelter.
5. Fill backpacks with school supplies for a

struggling school.

6. Gather and donate toiletries, make-up, and new underwear for a local women's shelter or human trafficking ministry.

7. Gather hats, scarves, and gloves for elementary school students in an impoverished community.

8. Hold a book drive for a local elementary school in need.

9. Hold a clothing drive for a local clothes closet ministry – or start your own!

10. Hold a diaper drive for your local pregnancy ministry.

11. Host a baby shower for a local pregnancy center to help them restock supplies for pregnant and new mothers.

12. Pack and distribute Thanksgiving Baskets (stuffing, mashed potatoes, canned veggies, cranberry sauce) for families in need.

13. Plan an Operation Christmas Child Packing Party for your neighborhood, church, or Bible study group.

14. Purchase presents for a local Angel Tree.

15. Send college care packages.

16. Send military care packages.

17. Send missionary care packages.

18. Sponsor a family at a local school for Christmas.

Random Acts of Kindness

1. Deliver bags of groceries, firewood, or gift cards to a local family in need.

2. Host a block party in a community near your church.

3. Leave bottles of bubbles at the park for families to use.

4. Leave quarters and washing detergent at your local laundromat.

5. Pass out water bottles to construction workers on a hot day.

6. Purchase coloring books and crayons and leave them in hospital waiting rooms/urgent care.
7. Set up a water/diaper changing station at an outdoor craft fair
8. Tape quarters or dollar bills to the vending machines in the waiting room of your local hospital.

Volunteer Your Time

1. Add some beauty and fresh landscaping to a school.
2. Adopt a classroom at a school with low test scores.
3. Bingo at a senior center
4. Cheer at a Special Olympics or special needs sports event.
5. Christmas carol at a nursing home or children's hospital.
6. Clean the home of an elderly person or homebound member of your church or community.
7. Clean the roadside – consider adopting a highway near your church.
8. Find a local field or farm that allows folks to glean.
9. Nursing home visits
10. Organize a blood drive.
11. Organize a free car care clinic for single moms in your community.
12. Plan a Habitat for Humanity workday.
13. Plant bulbs at your church or a local school
14. Rake leaves at a homebound member's house.
15. Take care of some yard work or handyman chores for one of the widows in your church or community.
16. Take communion to homebound church members.
17. Take on a Meals on Wheels route.
18. Visit a nursing home and host a game of Bingo.

19. Volunteer at a local women's shelter, homeless shelter, or another ministry in need.
20. Volunteer to clean and organize the food and your local food pantry.
21. Volunteer to help a refugee family complete paperwork, register for school, etc.
22. Work a shift at the local soup kitchen.

SPORTS

When we think of sports-related fellowship events, we often assume it's a men's ministry event. However, women love sports too! Poll your women to find out what types of sports they like to play and what types of sporting events they like to attend.

Don't limit yourself to professional teams – consider your local high schools too. Speak with your Youth Pastor to find out what sports the teens at your church play and go to one of their games to cheer them on!

Attending Sporting Events

1. Baseball Game
2. Basketball Game
3. Football Game
4. Hockey Game
5. Rodeo

Playing Sports/Exercise

1. Christian exercise class
2. Golf
3. Hiking
4. Horseback riding
5. Ice skating
6. Kayaking
7. Nature walk
8. Paddle boarding
9. Pickleball
10. Pilates
11. Putt-Putt
12. Roller skating
13. Self-defense class

14. Snow skiing
15. Snow tubing
16. Walking
17. Water park
18. Water skiing
19. Water tubing
20. Zumba

SPRING FELLOWSHIP IDEAS

Many women's ministry teams choose to honor mothers by hosting a Mother's Day event. Please be sensitive to include the women who want to be included. Those experiecing infertiltiy may want to avoid any and all Mother's Day activities. Most adoptive moms don't want to be singled out. Please tread carefully, keeping in mind that private acknowledgments are generally preferred over public ones.

1. Christian Passover meal
2. Easter craft
3. Easter-focused prayer stations
4. Easter-focused worship night
5. Flower arranging
6. Garden party
7. Garden tour
8. Plant bulbs or flowers at your church or for a homebound church member
9. Spring tea
10. Spring wreath
11. St. Patrick celebration (Christian missionary)

SUMMER FELLOWSHIP IDEAS

Summer doesn't have to mean more work for your team:
Keep things simple.

- Take advantage of parks, lakes, and other recreation areas.
- Minimize your planning by attending a festival or event nearby.

Most of these ideas take advantage of the warmer summer temperatures. However, if you live in an area where it's unbearably hot during the day, you may want to plan your activities for the evening when it's cooler.

1. Baseball game
2. BBQ/Cook-out
3. Bike
4. Boat tour
5. Catch a concert in the park
6. Concert
7. Craft festival
8. Day trip to the beach
9. Day trip to the mountains
10. Farmer's market
11. Food festival
12. Food tour
13. Garden party
14. Garden tour
15. Golf
16. Hiking
17. Ice cream social
18. Kayak
19. Music in the park

20. Nature trail
21. Outdoor movie (someone's home, drive-in, or local venue)
22. Outdoor play or musical
23. Paddleboard
24. Pedicure party
25. Pickleball
26. Play tourist and explore the top tourism spots in your city
27. Pool party
28. Stroll and shop along a street with cute boutiques
29. Shop and stroll
30. Strawberry/Blueberry Picking
31. Theme park
32. Thrift store shopping
33. Walking progressive dinner
34. Waterpark

WHAT DOES THE BIBLE SAY ABOUT _____?

These fellowship meetings could be led by one of your pastors, an expert on the topic, a pre-selected panel, or if you have a skilled emcee they could lead a small group discussion (I'd suggest no more than 15 women). The goal is to teach women to view everything through a biblical lens.

When applicable, don't neglect the importance of pointing women to a biblical counselor or medical doctor (be careful not to offer medical advice).

Topic ideas:

1. Abortion
2. Anger
3. Anxiety
4. Depression
5. Discipline
6. Divorce
7. Forgiveness
8. Gender
9. Gossip
10. Heaven
11. Holiness
12. Homosexuality
13. Honesty
14. Hope
15. Joy
16. Marriage
17. Money
18. Sanctification
19. Sex
20. Sin
21. Singleness
22. Submission
23. Widows
24. Wisdom
25. Women

WINTER FELLOWSHIP IDEAS

While we may not wish to promote New Year's resolutions (more often worldly-focused than biblically focused in attempt and target), we can encourage women to learn and strengthen holy habits in the new year. Valentine's day also lends itself to focusing on sharing God's love with others.

1. Basketball game
2. Bible study workshop
3. Blankets of love – create or collect for the homeless or a shelter
4. Cards of encouragement for single moms
5. Coat/sock collection for a local shelter
6. Escape room
7. Hockey game
8. Homeless blessing bags
9. Ice skating
10. Movie night
11. Prayer workshop
12. RAOK – Random acts of kindness spreading God's love
13. Scripture memory workshop
14. Soup swap
15. Valentine cards and candy outreach on college campuses
16. Valentine cookie or candy workshop
17. Valentine craft
18. Valentine's Day gift exchange
19. Valentine's day gifts for homebound

WORKSHOPS

I love this type of fellowship for three reasons:

1. It relies on the talents and skills of the women in your church and gets women involved that might not be your regular "women's ministry" attendees.
2. Everyone has the opportunity to learn a new skill. Participants experience Titus 2 in action.
3. Every person goes home with something! (That could include a sample, detailed directions, or a recipe.)

I recommend pre-registering women for the workshops so your team will know exactly how many supplies to purchase. You may want to offer options at two different price points as well.

1. Automotive basics (how to change the oil or a tire)
2. Basic sewing skills (button, hemming)
3. Bible journaling
4. Budgeting
5. Calligraphy
6. Canning (vegetable, fruit, or jam)
7. Creative lettering
8. Crochet/knitting
9. Cross-stitch
10. Door hangers
11. Etching
12. Freezer cooking
13. Gardening
14. Gift wrapping
15. Holiday-specific craft
16. How to make a no-sew fleece blanket
17. How to make a pie crust
18. How to make pasta from scratch

19. How to use chalk paint (furniture, mirrors, décor)
20. Make and take DIY cleaners
21. Painting
22. Photography
23. Pizza making
24. Tree decorating
25. Weaving
26. Wreath making

ADDITIONAL RESOURCES

You'll find additional resources for rethinking fellowship on the Women's Ministry Toolbox website (www.womensministrytoolbox.com) and the Women's Ministry Toolbox store (www.womensministrytoolboxshop.com).

Leaders have also found these Women's Ministry Toolbox resources helpful when developing their ministry plans:

- Women's Ministry Event Planning Course
  www.womensministrytraining.com

- READ Bible Study Kit for Groups
  www.readbiblestudy.com

- Prayer Warrior Boot Camp
  www.prayerwarriorbootcamp.com

ABOUT THE AUTHOR

 CYNDEE OWNBEY SERVES AS A mentor to thousands of women's ministry leaders through her website and Facebook community, Women's Ministry Toolbox. Drawing from over twenty years of experience ministering to women, Cyndee shares tried-and-true women's ministry tips and ideas that equip leaders to cultivate Christ-focused community. Having served in five different churches, Cyndee is able to relate to a variety of ministry situations and challenges.

Cyndee's best-selling book *Rethinking Women's Ministry: Biblical, Practical Tools for Cultivating a Flourishing Community* is the go-to resource for today's women's ministry leaders. Rethinking Women's Ministry invites leaders to take a fresh look at their ministry framework through the lens of Scripture and prayer.

Cyndee enjoys training women's ministry leaders and teaching at women's events and conferences whenever the opportunity allows. Cyndee and her husband have two sons and one daughter-in-law. They are enjoying life as empty-nesters in Charlotte, NC.

ADDITIONAL BOOKS

BY CYNDEE OWNBEY

Rethinking Women's Ministry: Biblical, Practical Tools for Cultivating a Flourishing Community

Rethinking Women's Ministry invites leaders to take a fresh look at their women's ministry framework through the lens of Scripture and prayer. Cyndee tackles the common obstacles women's ministry leaders face: generational gaps, unwilling mentors, biblical illiteracy, cliques, social media, sacred cows, and more! Using real-life, practical examples and easy-to-adopt strategies, *Rethinking Women's Ministry* gives leaders tools to develop a women's ministry that flourishes! Learn more at www.rethinkingwomensministry.com.

Rethinking Women's Ministry Workbook

In this companion to *Rethinking Women's Ministry: Biblical, Practical Tools for Cultivating a Flourishing Community*, seasoned women's ministry leader Cyndee Ownbey invites women's ministry leaders and teams to prayerfully evaluate their events, activities, mission, and structure.

With guided worksheets and exercises for each book chapter, Cyndee provides the tools you need to expand the reach of your ministry and accelerate the spiritual growth of the women in your church. Learn more at www.rethinkingwomensministry.com.

READ: A Bible Study Plan for Unpacking God's Word

The READ Bible study format breaks down common Bible study barriers with easy-to-follow, step-by-step instructions. Discover a daily Bible study routine that works!

READ: A Bible Study Plan for Unpacking God's Word is specifically designed to help you study God's Word on your own using a simple four-part process – Record, Explore, Apply, and Do.

In less than 20 minutes a day, you'll learn how to study God's Word on your own with confidence, develop healthy Bible study habits, go deeper in your time with God, and use resources to enhance your learning. Learn more at www.readbiblestudy.com.

Savor the Savior: A 21-Day Journey Through John

This 21-day journey through the book of John will warm your soul as you discover (or rediscover) who Jesus is through the eyes of John, Jesus' beloved disciple.

Included in this devotional book are daily scripture readings, reflection questions, daily prayers, and space for notes. Perfect for personal and small group Bible study. Learn more at www.savorthesavior.com.

END NOTES

1. Merriam-Webster. "Fellowship". https://www.merriam-webster.com/dictionary/fellowship.

2. GotQuestions.org. "What is the importance of Christian fellowship?", https://www.gotquestions.org/Christian-fellowship.html.

3. Strong LL.D., S.T.D., James. *The New Strong's Expanded Exhaustive Concordance of the Bible.* "Greek Dictionary of the New Testament". 2001. 141.

4. Keener, Craig S. *The IVP Bible Background Commentary New Testament.* 2014. 325.

5. Keener. The IVP *Bible Background Commentary New Testament.* 325.

6. Keener. The IVP *Bible Background Commentary New Testament.* 325.

7. Wiersbe, Warren W. *The Wiersbe Bible Commentary: New Testament.* 2007. 329.

8. Patterson, Dorothy Kelley and Kelley, Rhonda Harrington (editors). *Women's Evangelical Commentary: New Testament.* 2006. 264.

9. Barna Group. "A Biblical Worldview Has a Radical Effect on a Person's Life." https://www.barna.com/research/a-biblical-worldview-has-a-radical-effect-on-a-persons-life/)

10. Barna Dr., George. "American Worldview Inventory

2021." https://www.arizonachristian.edu/wp-content/
uploads/2021/08/CRC_AWVI2021_Release06_
Digital_01_20210831.pdf)

11. A similar list appears in my book, *Rethinking Women's Ministry* (139-145), however, I've made some important updates as I studied this idea through the lens of Acts 2. I'm always rethinking ministry too.

12. Wiersbe. *The Wiersbe Bible Commentary: New Testament.* 329.

13. Merida, Tony. *Christ-Centered Exposition: Exalting Jesus in Acts.* 2017. 40-41.

14. Merida. *Christ-Centered Exposition: Exalting Jesus in Acts.* 40.

15. Merida. *Christ-Centered Exposition: Exalting Jesus in Acts.* 40.

16. Merida. *Christ-Centered Exposition: Exalting Jesus in Acts.* 42.

17. Merriam-Webster. "Testimony." https://www.merriam-webster.com/dictionary/testimony.

Made in the USA
Middletown, DE
08 November 2023

42220849R00057